WIZARDS

Wizards

An Amazing Journey *through the*
Last Great Age of Magic

CANDACE SAVAGE

GREYSTONE BOOKS
Douglas & McIntyre Publishing Group
Vancouver/Toronto/New York

The author gratefully acknowledges the support of the Canada Council for the Arts in completing this project.

02 03 04 05 06   5 4 3 2 1

Greystone Books
A division of Douglas & McIntyre Ltd.
2323 Quebec Street, Suite 201
Vancouver, British Columbia
Canada V5T 4S7
www.greystonebooks.com

National Library of Canada Cataloguing in Publication Data

Savage, Candace, 1949-
   Wizards

Includes bibliographical references and index.
ISBN 1-55054-943-X

   1. Magic—History—Juvenile literature. 2. Wizards—Juvenile
literature. I. Title.
BF1589.S28 2002 j133.4'3'09032   C2002-910287-1

Editing by Linda Biesenthal
Jacket illustration by Rene Bull
Jacket and text design by Gabi Proctor/DesignGeist
Printed and bound in Hong Kong by C&C Offset Limited
Printed on acid-free paper

We gratefully acknowledge the financial support of the Canada Council for the Arts, the British Columbia Ministry of Tourism, Small Business and Culture, and the Government of Canada through the Book Publishing Industry Development Program (BPIDP) for our publishing activities.

Every attempt has been made to trace accurate ownership of copyrighted visual material. Errors and omissions will be corrected in subsequent editions, provided notification is sent to the publisher. See page 79 for a list of picture credits.

Illustrations: The illustration on the endpapers comes from the 1500s or 1600s. It shows a man poking his head right through the starry sky to find out about the mysteries that lie on the other side. Wizards were always searching for secret knowledge. The painting opposite the title page shows a sorcerer reciting phrases from his magical books, as he conjures up animal-like demons and an angel. It dates from 1825.

CONTENTS

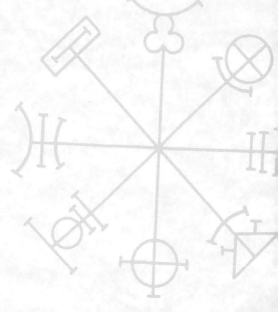

THE BOY WIZARD

When you grow up would you like to be
A master of magic and wizardry?

No one bothered to paint a portrait of Isaac Newton when he was a boy. But years later, after he had become famous, someone decided that this is what he must have looked like when he was young.

Isaac Newton began his training as a wizard when he was twelve years old. Like a real-life Harry Potter, he had lost his parents when he was very young. (His father died, his mother abandoned him, and he was forced to stay with relatives whom he detested.) But then, a few months before his thirteenth birthday in 1655, his fortunes began to improve—he was sent away to start school. King's Grammar School in the village of Grantham, England, was no Hogwarts: there were no classes in Divination or Defence Against the Dark Arts. There was not even any mathematics, which Isaac would have loved, just hour after hour of ancient Greek and Latin. But when classes were finally over, life began to hum.

Isaac boarded with a family who ran a kind of drugstore called an apothecary shop. From the outside, the shop looked like every other business along the cobbled street, a tall, narrow building with dingy windows and a creaking signboard. But inside, it was a treasure house of wonders from around the world. One wall was lined with drawers full of gray-

Facing page: This picture of an apothecary shop was made in the 1500s. It shows the apothecary behind his counter, grinding and mixing a tub of mysterious ingredients. The men on the right have come bustling in to buy a potion.

Mufcus, Camphora, Ambra.

The Language of Magic

Learning to read the ancient languages of Greek and Latin was the first step in the education of a wizard. By the 1600s, people had already been practicing magic for two or three thousand years. Over the centuries, some of the leading wizards had recorded their thoughts and observations in books, which were written in Greek and Latin. As an adult, Isaac Newton collected a large number of books about magic, with titles like *Secrets Reveal'd, Of Occult Philosophy* and *The Compound of Alchymy; or the Twelve Gates Leading to the Discovery of the Philosophers Stone.*

Isaac Newton (later Sir Isaac Newton) lived from 1642 until 1727. Although he dedicated much of his life to the study of magic, he is best known as one of the world's greatest mathematicians and scientists. In this illustration, he is using a prism to study the nature of light.

green herbs—chamomile, sage and thyme—that filled the air with the dusty smell of summer. Beside them were jars of spices from the distant Orient that gave off the sweet, exotic perfume of cloves and cinnamon. Nearby were wooden boxes filled with wolves' teeth, bears' fat, bats' wings and the shriveled carcasses of serpents.

Isaac and the apothecary's family lived in an apartment right above the shop. At night, Isaac fell asleep amid the strange, mingled odors of mint, sulfur and dried newts that wafted up through the floorboards. By day, he loved to crouch behind the long wooden counter in the shop and watch as Mr. Clark, the apothecary, weighed out the ingredients for making his magical remedies. Wide-eyed with curiosity, the boy recorded the recipes in his notebook. "To treat cuts, take a pinch of mint, a pinch of wormwood (a bitter herb), and 300 dried millipedes from which the heads have been removed. Grind this up in a mortar and add the resulting powder to four gallons of fermenting beer. Pour off a portion of this liquid and drink it two or three times a day, until the wounds are healed."

Isaac was the kind of child who liked to know how things worked. When a windmill was built in the district, he constructed a scale model that actually turned. (On days when the wind wasn't blowing, he powered his mill by putting a mouse on an exercise wheel.) Fascinated by the daily passage of the sun, he built a set of sundials and placed them all over the Clarks' cramped apartment—in his bedroom, in the kitchen, in the entrance hall, anywhere the sunbeams streamed in. He even pounded wooden pegs into the walls so that he could time the movement of the light around the rooms. As sunlight and shadow swirled across the walls, he imagined the sun and planets slowly swirling through the heavens. There was a secret order to the

Oil of Red Dog

In the 1500s and 1600s, a remedy called Oil of Red Dog was prescribed for people who had shriveled or lame arms. The recipe called for the body of one red-haired dog, 80 to 100 scorpions, a large dishful of ground worms, a handful of leaves from a plant called St. John's Wort and quantities of several other spices and herbs. These were all placed in a kettle of beer and simmered until the juices were thoroughly combined. The mixture was then strained and applied to the weakened limb. According to one apothecary, this potion had "infinite" powers.

As his potion steams and bubbles on the fire, an apothecary
drops in the final, magical touch—a dried scorpion.
Apothecaries sometimes also used a special kind of moss that
grew only on human skulls, like the one in the bottom left of
this illustration.

universe, Isaac sensed, and he was buzzing with desire to understand it.

The boy must have listened intently whenever Mr. Clark spoke about the hidden forces that he used in his potions and charms. A lump of coral, for instance, might look like nothing more than a dull orange-red stone, but it had the power to stop bleeding. A pinch of cumin seeds—ordinary, ridged, brown seeds—could be slipped into a potion to make people fall in love. A spoonful of powdered emeralds (bright as a twinkling eye) had the power to improve a person's eyesight. These healing powers were mysterious, Mr. Clark said, but they were also surprisingly ordinary. Magic was a fact of nature, like the sun and stars. For centuries, people had been using the powers hidden in stones, seeds and other everyday things to win love, treat diseases and solve other difficulties.

In the 1600s, the power of magic was as strong as ever before, and everyone in town—young and old, rich and poor—relied on Mr. Clark and his healing arts. But exactly what were the magical forces that made his remedies work? Were they spirits or some kind of invisible rays? Did different substances work their magic in the same, or different, ways? What was it about cumin or emeralds or millipedes that gave them their special powers? Why had God hidden these forces in the natural world? Did He want us to discover and use them to make our lives better? Would someone, someday, find the key that unlocked all the secrets of the universe?

The Royal Art of Magic

In the 1500s and 1600s, the magical arts were an accepted part of everyday life, not only in Grantham, England, but everywhere in Europe. From the poorest beggar to the greatest king or queen, everyone believed in the power of magicians to treat illness, foresee the future and achieve other useful results. For example, King Henry VIII of England, who reigned from 1509 to 1547, was a skilled apothecary, who spent his spare time mixing up potions and salves. His daughter Queen Elizabeth I, who was on the throne from 1558 to 1603, had a magic ring that she wore to protect herself against poisoning. And Charles I, who was the king when Isaac Newton was born, believed that he could cure epilepsy and skin diseases just by brushing people with his fingers. People flocked to him by the thousands to receive the king's magical touch.

There was no point in putting these questions to Mr. Clark. He was just a humble apothecary, not a philosopher. Although he could whip up a potion to cure your aches and pains, he did not have a deep understanding of God's secret plans. If Isaac wanted answers, he would have to find them for himself. And he certainly couldn't count on his relatives for help. They were practical, grim-faced people who had no patience with his endless questions and dreams. What he needed to do, they told him, was to finish school as quickly as possible, get back home and concentrate on doing something useful. He was going to be a farmer, and what did a farmer need to know about hidden forces and secret worlds?

But Isaac was transfixed by the mysteries that he had glimpsed in Mr. Clark's shop. When his family took him out of school in 1659, he reluctantly went through the motions of learning how to farm. But his heart wasn't in his duties, and every time he had a chance, he crept away to Grantham, slipped through the door of the apothecary shop and buried his nose in one of Mr. Clark's old, leather-bound books. If anyone had bothered to ask him about his ambitions, we can guess what he would have said. When he grew up, he was going to study the invisible powers at work in the universe. He was going to become a great wizard.

Facing page: John Dee's enemies said that he was an evil magician who used his powers to raise the dead. In this illustration, he and his friend Edward Kelley are shown in a graveyard, conjuring up a ghost. There is no evidence that they actually tried to do this.

The English magus John Dee believed that he could communicate with angels who appeared in mirrors and crystal balls. He was also an expert on geography and navigation.

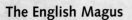

The English Magus

A great wizard—a person with a deep understanding of the hidden universe—was sometimes referred to as a magus. And one of the greatest magi of all times was an Englishman named John Dee, who lived from 1527 until 1608. A brilliant and educated man, he was an expert on a wide range of subjects, including geography, map-making, navigation, mathematics, lenses, fortune-telling, finding buried treasure, astrology and the language of angels. In later life, he spent every penny he had on a search for the philosopher's stone (more about this later). Although he died about thirty-five years before Isaac Newton was born, he was remembered in Isaac's time as both a magician and a scholar.

THE DARK ARTS

Fire burn and cauldron bubble—

Demons cause a lot of trouble.

Deciding to become a wizard was an important first step in choosing a career. But exactly what kind of magic did the would-be wizard wish to pursue? Would he stick with healing magic, like his friend Mr. Clark? Or might he be tempted to become a follower of the Dark Arts?

The Dark Arts were the realm of the devil. Today, we think of the devil—if we think of him at all—as a fellow in a red jump-suit with a pointed tail and horns. But in the 1600s, the devil was lurking in every shadow. He was the force of evil that caused things to go wrong. When a baby died (and so many died), it was the devil's fault. When a cow took sick and couldn't stand up, when gardens were flattened by hail, when people went hungry (as they often did), these were all signs that the devil had been busy.

The devil was assisted in this wicked work by a huge company of evil spirits, or demons. (In 1462, one expert stated that the world was inhabited by

This gloomy-looking creature is a demon, an evil spirit who, it was said, went around the world causing pain and torment (even to himself).

Facing page: Under the ghostly light of a full moon, two sorcerers have gone out into the forest and conjured up a demon (the nasty-looking presence on the right). They have called him by reciting magical words from their book of spells.

Care of Magical Pets

In the early 1600s, an old woman lived in a lonely cottage outside Newmarket in eastern England. Her only companion was a pet toad that lived under her chest of drawers. When the woman made a special chuckling sound, the toad would hop out and accept a drink of milk from a saucer. The woman believed that the toad was a demon, or "familiar spirit," that gave her the power to work magic.

exactly 126,792 evil spirits.) There were demons of the air, earth and water; demons large and small; demons that appeared in the shape of ravens, cats, bears, hares, bees and dogs. One woman said she had met a demon who looked like a gentleman dressed all in black, but with feet like a cow's. Another complained that she had become seriously ill after swallowing a demon that was hiding under a lettuce leaf in her salad.

Right: This demon is cute, but don't be fooled. He is probably hatching some plot to trouble the world.

Above: A priest (the man in the gown on the left) uses holy wine and bread to chase a demon out of a sick woman. The man on the right is holding her so that she can be helped. The illustration dates from 1598.

Mother Midnight

Although demons could look amusing, they were not good company. For one thing, they could leave you with terrible dreams or literally drive you crazy. In the 1600s, people who suffered from mental illness were thought to have been invaded, or "possessed," by evil spirits. Even worse, demons might persuade a person to forsake God and join in the devil's work. Despite his thousands of demon-helpers, the devil was always looking for new recruits. And he was ready to make a tempting offer to anyone who was willing to join him. If a person promised to help cause suffering and pain, the devil would reward him or her with the power to work magic. Black Magic.

People in the 1600s were familiar with two kinds of evil magicians. First, there were witches. Everyone

Left: Two witches stuff a serpent and a rooster into their cauldron as they brew up an evil spell. As a result of their magic, the sky is darkened by a hail storm that will flatten gardens and crops.

Facing page: In 1498, when this picture was drawn, witches were thought to have the power to turn into animals. These three witches have partially transformed themselves into a donkey, a bird and a sheep, before zooming off into the night on their flying stick.

Facing page, background: If a person believed that he or she had fallen under a spell, there was an easy answer. Just make a fist with the thumb tucked under the second finger, and the spell would be broken.

agreed that witches were mostly women—old, bent crones—with wrinkles, warts, hairy lips and screeching voices. They were constantly angry and loved to complain and curse. But they weren't just grumpy old women. They were servants of the devil, so everyone said, and their angry words had a frightening power to cause trouble. Everyone had a story about the time when old Granny So-and-So had shouted, "I hope your horse drops dead" (just because someone had refused to give her a ride into town), and the very next day, the horse had been found, lying still and cold, in the pasture. A witch's curse was fearful, people said, because she had made a deal, or "pact," with the devil. In fact, all her magical powers—her ability to turn herself into an animal or fly through the night on a broom—came from this same, dreadful source. The witch was a practitioner of the Dark Arts.

The second type of evil magician was the sorcerer. Typically a man, the sorcerer usually followed some respectable profession by day; he might be a tailor or a shopkeeper or, surprisingly often, a clergyman. But under cover of darkness, he shed his respectable clothes and pulled on the long, flowing gown of a magician. Then, laden with sacks of gear and looking nervously from left to right, he tiptoed out of town, past sleeping cottages, to the most secret part of the forest. There he pulled out his heavy book of

Witch Bottles

Witches were often suspected of making people sick. One popular cure in such cases was to prepare a "witch bottle." This was a fat-bellied pottery jug that was filled with the patient's urine and a few other choice items, such as pins and threads that were tied up in knots. This concoction was placed beside the kitchen hearth, where it was allowed to simmer and steam for hours. When the witch who had caused the disease felt the fire's heat, the pin pricks and the knot-like cramps, she was expected to give up and remove her enchantment. Whenever anyone got better, it was taken as proof that the witch bottle had done its work.

spells, turned the key in its lock and began to follow the instructions for conjuring up demons. (Since girls and women weren't allowed to go to school, they couldn't learn to read and weren't often tempted to study sorcery.)

The sorcerer's secret book was filled with complicated instructions for what were called "experiments." As one might expect from a book of evil magic, many of the projects were nasty. For instance, one sorcerer in the 1400s explained how to cause pain by making an ugly doll out of candle wax, putting someone's name on it and piercing it with pins. Another section described a method for causing a fight between friends by enchanting two stones, smashing and bashing them together and filling them with crabby demons.

Losers Weepers

On January 28, 1510, four English sorcerers (a teacher, two parsons and a priest) went out into the woods to conjure up evil spirits. They hoped the demons would help them find buried treasure. Instead, the sorcerers got lost in the fog and barely found their way home! When news of their misadventure leaked out, they were all arrested. Practicing Black Magic was against the law and could be punished with a jail term or even death.

Right: In the 1500s and 1600s, more than 50,000 people were hanged or burned as witches in western Europe. Like the three shown dangling here in 1589, most of the people convicted of witchcraft were women.

Facing page: In the flickering gloom of midnight, a wizard (Alcandre by name) has drawn his magic circle and inscribed mystical symbols in the dirt. Now, he is reciting magical phrases to call demons from the shadows. This illustration dates from 1626.

A Pocketful of Trouble

To become invisible, magicians were sometimes advised to carry fern seed in their pockets. To be effective, the seed had to be collected on the night of the summer solstice, June 21. One man who went out to gather seeds said that he had been harassed by spirits that whizzed past his ears, bumped into his hat and emptied all his carefully folded seed packages.

But sorcerers weren't always black-hearted. In more playful moods, they used their powers to set the world alight with wonder. If the spell books were to be believed, a skilful sorcerer could conjure up a castle, complete with knights in armor and a deep moat (unfortunately, the whole scene would fade away after three or four hours). Or he could produce a banquet with a thousand types of dishes, which everyone present would find delicious. Instructions were also given for conjuring up spirit horses, magic ships and flying thrones.

There were even ways to become invisible. To obtain a cloak of invisibility, for example, the sorcerer was instructed to wait for a clear Wednesday evening—no other time would do—when the moon was waning from full to new. At 1 a.m., he was to sneak out to the forest dressed in a white robe, carrying a supply of incense and a splendid sword. Choosing a level piece of ground, he was to draw a circle in the dirt with the tip of his sword. Around this circle, he would then write the names of four particular demons: Firiel (to the west), Melemil (to the south), Berith (to the east) and Taraor (to the north). When this was done, the sword was to be placed on the name of Firiel.

Next, the sorcerer was to walk round the circle, starting in the west, carrying his pot of incense. Then, kneeling and facing to the east, he was to call out in a loud voice: "I, so-and-so [he'd say his name], conjure you, O Firiel, Melemil, Berith and Taraor, powerful, magnificent, illustrious spirits, that all four of you should come here with utmost humility, bound, constrained, and sworn to carry out my command, whatever I ask of you. Come without delay." This was to be repeated three more times, facing south, east and north, once for each of the demons.

As soon as this ceremony had been completed—or so the spell book said—the demons would appear inside the magic circle. The sorcerer was then to tell them what they were to do: "I wish a cloak of invisibility, which should be thin and incorruptible, so that when I wear it no one can see me or sense my presence." Immediately, one of the spirits would leave and return with the cloak. Apparently, it was that simple!

The appeal of Black Magic was obvious. By agreeing to cooperate with the devil, a sorcerer gained the power to control tremendous forces and work wonders. But in the process, he joined the side of evil—of suffering, madness and death. Some people were willing to accept the devil's bargain, but young Isaac Newton would never be one of them. Yes, a cloak of invisibility might have come in handy when he was sneaking away from the farm, but the moral price was unthinkable. He would never be seduced to the side of the devil. His mind was aflame with wonder at the hidden powers he had seen in Mr. Clark's shop—secrets that were hidden by God in the natural world.

Old Women walk, fmoke and talk

Top: The pointed hat of the Hallowe'en witch was borrowed from the costume that country women wore during the 1500s and 1600s.

Bottom: Although most sorcerers were men, this woman has learned to read and turned her talents to sorcery.

Natural Magic

Any time you're feeling sick
A few dried bugs should do the trick.

Black Magic was the art of working wonders with the help of demons. Natural Magic (the kind that Mr. Clark practiced) was the art of performing miracles using the powers hidden in ordinary things. Even the most common, everyday objects—a pocketful of colored stones, a bowl of dried flowers, a lump of wax drained from someone's ear—could have unexpected abilities. An apothecary was a natural magician who used these hidden "virtues," or strengths, to treat discomfort and disease. Suppose, for example, that a girl showed up at Mr. Clark's door with a terrible toothache. She could have gone to the blacksmith and had the tooth yanked out, but the thought of his big, black pliers was more than she could bear. Couldn't the apothecary do something to help? And so Mr. Clark would do his best to assist her. For example, he might prescribe a charm— a magical chant or verse—that the girl could recite to herself. Or he might write those same words on a piece

An apothecary and two assistants prepare medicines, sometime in the 1500s or 1600s. The woman on the right is sorting and drying medicinal herbs, while the other two are making potions.

Facing page: A sick girl droops on her seat as she waits for the wizard to diagnose her illness. He is looking for clues in a flask of her urine.

Xyloaloes.   Mufcus.   Camphora.   Ambra.   AquaRofa.   Syrupusacetofus.   Syrupus.

Now that is devilish stomach ache! If an illness was thought to be caused by demons, then the apothecary prescribed charms and herbs that drove the evil spirits away.

of paper and form them into a pendant, or amulet, for her to hang around her neck. In either case, the magical words were supposed to release an invisible force that would heal her pain.

If the charm didn't work, the apothecary might turn to healing plants, or herbs. Since no one had ever heard of germs, toothaches were thought to be caused by worms that burrowed into the jaw. Apparently, these tooth worms hated certain herbs, such as holly leaf, onion seed and sage. Armed with this valuable information, the apothecary would select a handful of leaves and seeds and throw them into a pot of water. When the mixture came to the boil, it was poured into a bowl, and the sufferer was told to sit in the steam, with mouth wide open. The worms would be so offended by this treatment that they would leap out of the patient's mouth, taking the toothache along with them.

Apothecaries used dozens of different plants, and each had its own secret powers. Potatoes and nutmeg, for example, were surprisingly useful in treating aches and pains. Although you could eat these foods if you wanted to, the treatment would also work if you simply carried a spud or a bottle of spice around in your pocket. It seemed that potatoes and nutmeg both produced magical rays that helped to keep the discomfort away. This idea—that herbs worked by chasing away sickness or by attracting good health—was known as the theory of "sympathies and antipathies," or attractions and hatreds. Some plants just naturally hated some sicknesses.

People didn't have much respect for doctors in the 1500s and 1600s. This cartoon shows a fat and foolish-looking doctor, wearing silly shoes and carrying a ridiculous flask. He is followed by his chubby assistant.

Doctor Leech

There were university-trained medical doctors in the 1600s, but only rich people could afford them. This wasn't as much of a problem as you might expect, since medicine was not very sophisticated. No matter what the disease, doctors were likely to prescribe one of three treatments: cutting the patient and draining away sick blood, applying leeches to suck the illness out or making the patient throw up. Faced with these options, many people greatly preferred to go to the apothecary or to a neighborhood "charmer" who practiced Natural Magic.

Of all the plants used to make healing potions, one of the most amazing was the mandrake. Because its roots looked a little like a pair of human legs, people imagined that the mandrake was a spirit-being. Legend had it that if this being were disturbed, it would scream so terribly that anyone who heard it would instantly die. Dogs, on the other hand, were not affected by the mandrake's high-pitched yowls, so they could be used to pull the precious roots out of the ground.

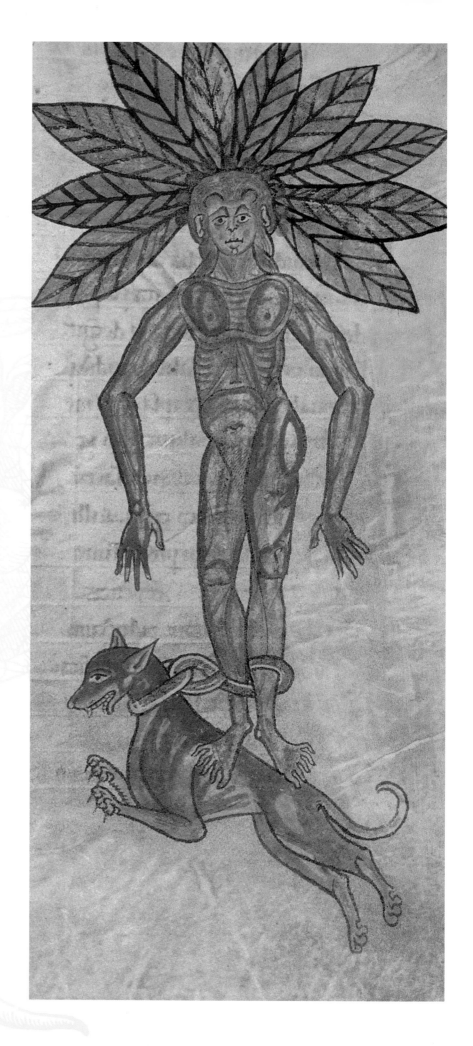

Sometimes, the secret powers of plants could only be uncovered by experimenting with them. Who would ever have guessed that a cup of mint tea or a handful of parsley leaves would help to settle a sick stomach? But often it was possible to figure out how a plant was meant to be used just by looking at it. The leaf of a rose, for example, is marked with a network of thin red veins, red as the blood in our own bodies. Surely, this was a clue that the rosebush could be used to treat disorders of the blood and circulatory system. A walnut, on the other hand, looks like a tiny, wrinkled brain inside a bony skull—proof positive that God had made it to cure headaches and brain ailments. A plant with milky sap would help a new mother to produce milk; one with strong fibrous stems would help a bone to set—and so it went. This theory was known as "the doctrine of signatures."

Chasing Away the Blues

In the 1600s, a herb called St. John's Wort was used in potions and charms to protect people from evil spirits. Today, this same herb has been scientifically proven to help people who are suffering from depression. It is sold in most pharmacies and health-food stores.

Flower Power

Wizards used to make potions from the foxglove flower and give them to people who were suffering from tuberculosis, or TB. They said that foxglove had a mysterious "virtue" that gave it the power to chase away disease. We know now that foxglove contains a powerful chemical called digitalis, which is used to treat people who have heart conditions.

Above: Mandrakes were said to come in two sexes, male and female.

Left: According to the doctrine of signatures, plants had been created for specific purposes that were "written" right into the plants' appearance. Here, for example, are plants for treating the tongue and the stomach.

In the 1600s, people believed that the natural world was filled with magic and medicine. Here, an apothecary mixes up a remedy, surrounded by the wonders of nature.

Left: A man harvests a magical stone from the head of a toad for use in making medicine.

Magical plants were not the only ingredients that apothecaries like Mr. Clark stored on their shelves. They also stocked bits and pieces of various animals, including ants' eggs, boars' teeth, crabs' eyes, donkeys' hooves, powdered worms, fish bones, goats' dung, dried serpents, jellied vipers and scorpions simmered in oil. Again, every preparation was believed to have its own specific magical powers. For example, frogs were caught, killed, cut up, dried and pounded into a powder, which was used to treat nosebleeds. Two different kinds of millipedes were also kept on hand: one sort was fat and bluish-black; the other was brown and flat with a wicked-looking forked tail. These insects were made into a powder or cooked into syrups and jams. But they were also fed—live and wriggling—to people who had asthma, at a rate of fifty millipedes per dose, four doses in twenty-four hours. There was nothing like swallowing a few hundred bugs to take your mind off your chest!

The apothecary stored his most precious treasures under his counter or up on his highest shelf. If a customer flashed him a little money, he would get them out—small packets of emeralds, pearls, silver and gold. Emeralds were said to be good for the liver and eyes; pearls were for poisoning; gold was a cure-all that drew its healing power from the sun. You could obtain all these benefits by wearing the gems around your neck as

Tried and True?

Many of the magical remedies that were used in the 1600s had been around for hundreds of years. They had been written down in ancient times by Greek and Roman scholars. If the Roman philosopher Pliny the Elder (who lived in the first century) said that stones from an eagle's nest had healing powers, then people accepted it. They thought that a wise man like Pliny could never be mistaken. And if the famous Greek physician Galen (another ancient scholar) said that you should grind up worms with pepper and spread them on your sore cheeks, then it was time to start grinding. In fact, many of the old remedies didn't work at all. When patients got better, it usually was because they had recovered on their own. But people liked the idea that they could do something to help themselves, and so they continued to use the old medicines.

The Mystery of the Unicorn

Although Europeans had seen unicorn horns, they had never seen the animal that grew that wonderful appendage. The horn was imported over the trade routes from Asia, and it passed through many hands on its long trip to the West. With every step in the journey, it became more mysterious. But sometime in the 1600s, the mystery was resolved. Unicorn horn turned out to be the tusk of the narwhal.

When the unicorn lost its mystery, it lost its magic as well. Unicorn horn had only worked (assuming that it sometimes did) because people believed in it. When that faith was gone, the magic disappeared too. In fact, faith was the first principle of most magical cures. The thingamabob that did the job wasn't really the bag of millipedes or the powdered pearls or even the magic words. It was the belief that the magic would work.

charms. But they seemed to work even better if you swallowed them. Precious stones were often smashed into tiny pieces, mixed with all kinds of other stuff, made into pills or potions—and then eaten.

One famous remedy, called Countess of Kent's Powder, was widely used in both England and France as a treatment for measles, smallpox and the plague. The recipe called for coral, amber and pearls in equal quantities. These were to be combined in a sturdy bowl with measured amounts of crabs' claws, dried snakes, saffron, jellied vipers and assorted herbs. The ingredients were then to be beaten with a mortar until they were reduced to dust, shaped into pills and put away in a cool, dry place until needed.

But the most valuable object in the apothecary shop was not a precious stone. It was the tusk of the unicorn. Slender and creamy white, a complete tusk might reach almost up to the roof, and every single ounce of it was worth its weight in gold. Even the tiniest flake, floated in wine, was said to have the power to cure a raging fever. The smallest pinch of powdered horn, made into a jelly, was reputed to make you feel happy and energetic. Most remarkable of all, unicorn horn was credited with the ability to counteract every known poison, from arsenic to snake venom.

Under the shriveled gaze of a dried crocodile, an apothecary brews up a remedy (far right), while three others mix and measure ingredients (center). At the left, a customer comes to the counter to pick up a remedy. This illustration was first published in 1722.

Isaac Newton was wonder-struck by the apothecary's art. Even when he was grown up and famous, he would continue to mix up batches of his favorite remedies and dose himself with them. (His standby was a concoction called Lucatello's Balsam that included beeswax, strong wine, sandalwood and turpentine—pure poison!) But his study of magical healing, as fascinating as it was, could not take him to the heart of the matter. If he wanted to understand the why's and wherefore's of the hidden universe, he was going to have to journey deeper.

Divination

Visionary and oracular—

Magic at its most spectacular!

Facing page: Some village wizards foretold the future. The famous Mother Shipton, shown on the right, lived from 1488 to 1561. She is credited with having predicted the invention of the automobile ("a carriage without a horse shall go") and even the Internet ("around the world men's thoughts shall fly quick as the twinkling of an eye").

Mr. Clark was probably not

the only magician whom Isaac Newton encountered during his years at school. In the 1600s, a good-sized village like Grantham would have had a full range of magical practitioners. But unlike the apothecary, who ran a shop with a sign-board swinging above the door, most of the other magicians were not so easy to recognize. They were just ordinary men and women— and, occasionally, even children—who had earned extraordinary reputations for making charms, mixing potions, breaking evil spells and providing other kinds of magical services. Although few of these people had been to school, they had learned their skills from their ancestors—their mothers, their grandfathers, their withered old uncles and aunts. Some of them seemed to understand mysteries that were far beyond a mere apothecary's grasp.

They could tell if someone was be-witched and how to break the spell; they knew the nature and cure of every ailment. And this remarkable gift of vision also let

Right: When their baby fell sick, this family called on the village wizard, or wise woman (left), for help.

What will the answer be? Everyone watches and waits as the village wizard comes out of her trance and prepares to make a dramatic announcement. Wizards could be called on to solve crimes, find lost objects and cure illnesses. The man on the right is probably hoping for help with his aching tooth.

them look into the mysteries of the past and the future. They could peer back in time and uncover secrets that had never been told. They could tell you what would happen tomorrow or in ten years or, if you cared, in five centuries.

The art of looking into the unknown world is called divination, and it was one of the standard services that was offered by village wizards. Although divination sounds exotic, its uses were surprisingly down-to-earth. Typically, the story began when something was stolen or lost—something valuable, like a sheep or a purse full of coins. No one could find the thing anywhere; it just seemed to have disappeared. Clearly, this was a job for the village wizard.

One of the simplest methods of finding lost objects—and the most popular—was called "divination by sieve and shears." As the name suggests, this technique required two pieces of equipment, a big, flat strainer, or sieve, and a huge pair of scissors, or shears. The first step in the procedure was simply to open the shears and hold them with the points up. Next, two people moved into position, to the right and left, so that each could grab hold of one of the open blades. The sieve was then placed on top of the shears and balanced there. As soon as it was sitting still, the divination could begin. As the wizard called out the places where the item

A village wizard has dealt a spread of cards to predict the fate of her two young clients. Although card reading depends mostly on intuition, certain cards have set meanings. For example, the ace of hearts signifies love and happiness, while the ace of spades warns of conflict and difficulty.

This girl has cut the peel off her apple in one, long twist, without breaking it. According to tradition, this is a sign that her wishes will come true.

might have been lost, everyone kept their eyes on the wobbly apparatus. If the sieve turned or trembled when a location was named, someone would run off to look for the missing object.

In the 1600s, people took divination by sieve and shears very seriously—so seriously, in fact, that they relied on it not only to find things but also to solve cases of theft. The basic method was the same, except that instead of listing places where the missing item might be, the wizard called out the names of people who were suspected of having snitched it. When the sieve teetered, it was taken as a sign that the thief had been identified. In fact, the shear-holders probably tipped the sieve themselves, in their excitement at naming the person whom they thought was responsible for the theft. The tiniest tremor of emotion was enough to upset the sieve and accuse the guilty party (or perhaps the innocent). If the wizard who conducted the divination had a reputation for success, the person named by the strainer might be put under arrest. Sometimes the accusations turned out to be mistaken, but surprisingly often they were correct. If you knew everyone in the village, you knew whom to suspect, whether or not your sieve and shears were psychic.

The sieve and shears could also be used to solve other mysteries. What is the name of my future husband? Does the red-haired girl love me? Is Mrs. So-and-So going to have a baby? Alternatively, these same questions could be put to another popular oracle —the key and book. This method of divination was

Whodunit?

Like the private detectives in mystery novels, village wizards were often called in to sort out clues and identify criminals. In 1618, for example, a diviner named Jane Bulkeley was hired to identify a thief from a list of ten suspects. Her technique was to cut a cheese into ten portions, write a charm on each of them and require each suspect to swallow one. Woe betide the person who choked on his or her lump! A guilty conscience can make for a very dry throat.

Do-It-Yourself Divination

If a girl wanted to know the name of her future husband, she could make her own investigations. All she had to do was locate a well that was on a main route to and from a church where weddings were held. She would dip her nightdress in the well and hang the garment to dry by the fire in her room. That night, the form of her true love would come to her in a dream or vision.

Surrounded by his leather-bound books and magical paraphernalia, a wizard conjures up a vision in his crystal ball. In this illustration, the artist has playfully supplied the wizard with three vials (lower left) labeled "Good Luck," "Elixir of Peace," and "Financial Extract."

Right: Some wizards claimed that they could read a person's character from the shape of his or her head. A person who looked like a cow, for example, was sure to be lazy and stupid.

usually performed with a Bible, a hymn book or some other big, heavy tome with a reputation for truthfulness. The book was opened to a chosen page (often one of the Psalms), and a key was laid on top of it. The wizard and his or her assistant then picked up this apparatus and, grasping it by the corners, held it as steady as they could. Again, questions were asked and possible answers proposed. Would it be Matthew, George or Harold? Yes or no? When the book jittered or jolted so that the key moved, it was a signal that the truth had been revealed.

Some wizards specialized in a more sophisticated technique for gaining secret knowledge. It was called scrying, and the people who practiced it were scryers. A scryer could see things that were happening at other places and times by gazing into a crystal ball. Light swirled through the hazy globe like curls of smoke, in a fluid, flowing dance of brightness and

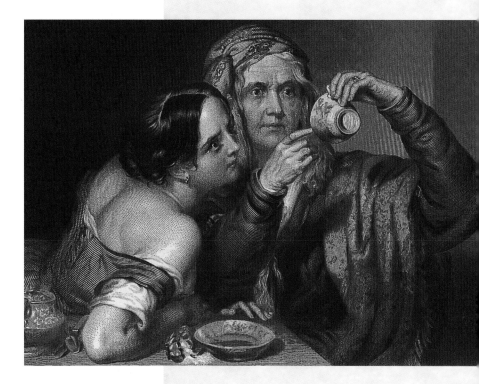

When tea is made with loose leaves rather than tea bags, leaves settle to the bottom of the cup. Once the tea has been drunk, the patterns made by the leaves can be interpreted. Here, a tea-leaf reader (the woman on the right) stares into the bottom of the cup to read the future of her client.

Clairvoyant Frogs

A village wizard named Joan Mores, who lived in Kent, England, around 1525, claimed that she could foretell the future by listening to the croaking of frogs. A couple of hundred years later, in the 1700s, other wizards made their predictions by "casting" coffee grounds and drawing whatever sense they could from the splodgy brown patterns. The idea of reading tea leaves, though much tidier, did not become popular until sometime later.

Many wizards believed that they could read their clients' characters or predict their futures simply by studying their appearance. By the 1800s, this idea had become the basis of an elaborate science called "phrenology." Phrenologists believed that they could tell absolutely everything about a person by measuring the bones and bumps on his or her skull.

shadow. Squint and you might see a missing cow, an unborn child or the train of a wedding dress. A wizard who had no crystal ball could seek for these same visions in a filmy old mirror or almost any other reflective surface. Some scryers claimed to see the faces of thieves swimming in basins of water or in murky horse troughs. Others could uncover the mysteries of the past and the future by gazing at a thumbnail. If the nail was coated with vegetable oil to give it a sheen, it became a miniature screen on which mini-apparitions could be seen.

Magic was at work in the simplest, most ordinary things. In particular, there was magic and meaning in every part of the human body. For example, the future was written in the lines on your palms and the wrinkles on your forehead. Wizards knew how to interpret these coded messages. If the curving line that bracketed your right thumb was long, you would live to a ripe old age. If it was short, you were fated to die young. A diagonal scar or crease above the left eye foretold a violent death, but a slash above your right eye marked you as adventurous. Buck teeth meant you were prone to fits of anger, and big lips made you a liar. Even the position of moles could be read as signs of the future. A mole near the eyebrow was the mark of a happy marriage, and one on the chin signaled wealth. But pity the poor person with a mole on the neck—he or she was destined to be beheaded!

Above right: This chart was made for telling fortunes by interpreting facial moles.

Signs of Things to Come

In the 1600s, many methods of divination were popular.

Aeromancy: interpreting clouds or rainbows

Auguria: making a prediction based on the behavior of birds

Biteromancy: divining the future from a person's name

Capnomancy: interpreting shapes that appear in smoke or mists

Geomancy: interpreting earthquakes

Physiognomy: judging a person's destiny from the shape of the head

Pedestria: predicting the future from the behavior of four-footed animals

Pyromancy: interpreting comets, northern lights and other fiery phenomena

Umbilicomancy: predicting how long a person would live by counting the bumps on his or her umbilical cord

With her little dog at her ankle and a purse dangling from her hand, a well-dressed woman bashfully approaches a fortune teller to have her palm read. This illustration was made in 1750.

People paid good money to have wizards read their moles, stare at their thumbs, and pose questions to clairvoyant sieves. A consultation often cost an entire day's wages. Yet people were willing to pay because they needed help. In the 1600s, there were no police services or insurance policies, no food banks or welfare checks. If you got sick, you either lived or died. If your cow was stolen, you went hungry for butter and milk. Life teetered on a knife-edge, between misery and happiness. By explaining why things happened, diviners gave people a sense that life was predictable—a magical illusion that they were happy to pay for.

But for a boy like Isaac Newton, the diviners' answers only served to raise more troubling questions. Was there some underlying reality that only wizards could sense? Could he ever hope to get a glimpse of the hidden world?

When someone put a spell on this man, he came to the local wizard for help. By gazing into her bucket of water, she has seen the face of the sorcerer who is responsible for the trouble. Now, she solemnly prepares to undo the evil magic by thrusting a knife into the water.

Left: Palm readers foretell the future by studying the lines on a person's hand. The Heart Line deals with relationships, the Head Line with intelligence, and the Life Line with health. For example, if a person has a deep, straight Head Line, a palm reader interprets that as a sign of practicality and intelligence.

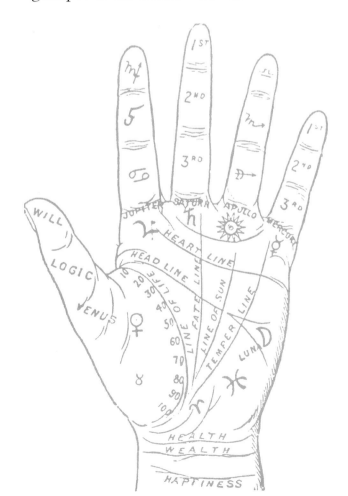

Made an error? Been a dope?

Blame it on your horoscope.

O f all the branches of magic, there was one that stood out from the rest. Nothing could top it for daring or scope or pure ambition. It was called astrology, and its aim was nothing less than to penetrate the deepest, most far-reaching mysteries of Earth and heaven. Isaac Newton first stumbled upon this subject quite by accident, when he picked up a book on astrology at a flea market. Could this tattered pamphlet lead him down the path to becoming a mighty magus?

Although we don't know the title or author of Isaac's astrology book, it might very well have been written by the most famous English wizard of the seventeenth century, an astrologer named William Lilly. Like Isaac, William was well acquainted with difficulty and frustration. From his birth in 1602, Lilly had been the pampered, only child of a well-to-do family. But by the time of his eighteenth birthday, his mother was dead and his father was lying in prison, deeply in debt. So, like a character in a fairy

Facing page: Michel de Nostradame, better known as Nostradamus, lived from 1503 until 1566. A doctor by training, he became famous for writing hundreds of quatrains (four-line poems) that predicted future disasters. He is seen here with two other astrologers, studying the planets and stars.

William Lilly, who lived from 1602 until 1681, is shown with his star globe, book of astrological symbols and a horoscope (under his left hand). In the 1600s, astrologers used a form like this one, marked off in triangles and squares, to work out their predictions.

tale, Lilly bought himself a new suit of clothes, borrowed a few pence from his friends and set out for London to seek his fortune. He arrived in the great city just in time to witness an outbreak of the plague. "The woeful Calamity of that Year was grievous," he later recalled. "People [lay] dying in the open Fields and in the open Streets." Yet not everyone in the city suffered this terrible fate. Some became ill and recovered; others—like Lilly himself—didn't get sick at all. Why were people's lives so different from one another?

Lilly sought for answers to this question in the occult arts. In particular, he was attracted to the idea that our lives are shaped by the influence of the heavens. We all know that the heavenly bodies give off visible light. But what if they also produce invisible rays that beam down through space? What if these invisible rays control our individual fate? These were the central ideas of astrology, the most powerful and far-reaching science in all of wizardry.

William Lilly wanted to know more, so in 1632 he signed up for private lessons with a wizard named Evans who lived on a street called Gun-Powder Alley in London. A squat, gnome-like man with a head of wild black curls, Evans had once been a respectable parson, but he had been thrown out of the church for

Three astrologers gaze out into a universe that is streaming with energy.

some kind of disgraceful behavior. When Lilly met him, he was earning his living by selling magical goblets that were supposed to cure flu, stomach aches, fevers, madness and intestinal worms. But Evans was also an experienced astrologer who, for a fee, was happy to share what he knew with Lilly.

The lessons began with the basics. The cosmos, Evans informed his student, consists of nine crystal spheres that are nested one inside the other. The innermost sphere contains Earth, which sits perfectly

At the center of the astrologers' universe sits Earth. Around it, in seven, nested crystal spheres, are the "wandering stars," or planets—the Moon, Mercury, Venus, the Sun, Mars, Jupiter and Saturn. At the outer limits of the cosmos are the "fixed stars," which trace out the constellations, or star signs, of the zodiac. This astrological calendar dates from about 1550.

still at the very center of the universe. Beyond Earth are seven more crystal globes, each one larger than the last. These globes hold the seven "wandering stars," or planets. (Since Neptune and Pluto were not known at the time, the planets included the Moon, Mercury, Venus, the Sun, Mars, Jupiter and Saturn.) Finally, in the farthest distance, we see the shining multitude of stationary, or "fixed," stars, which are studded like diamonds across the outer limits of the heavens.

This ninth and outermost wheel of stars is known as the zodiac. According to Evans (and to astrologers before and since), this great starry sphere is divided into twelve equal parts, which are arranged like the slices of a pie. Each slice is home to a particular constellation, or "star sign," a connect-the-dots image that is outlined with stars. Look up and you'll see them parading around the circumference of the night sky: Taurus the Bull, Aries the Ram, Gemini the Twins, Scorpio the Scorpion and all the rest, each in its special slot in the heavens.

According to astrologers, the planets and the stars affect our lives by zapping us with their invisible rays. Each of them influences us in its own special ways. If you are hit by rays from the planet Mercury, for instance, you will be filled with get-up-and-go. But if you're struck by the cold rays of Saturn, you can expect to feel miserable. Whether you are happy or sad, rich or poor, sick or well depends on which of the planets has you under its spell. The star signs, for their part, act like filters

Astrology and Astronomy

Astrology is concerned with the hidden, or occult, powers of the planets and stars. That is why it is classified as a magical, or occult, art. Astronomy, by contrast, concentrates on the physical characteristics of the heavenly bodies—how big they are, how fast they move and so on. Until the 1700s, the main purpose of studying astronomy was to obtain information that could be used in casting horoscopes.

A Revolutionary Idea

In 1543, Nicolas Copernicus argued that the sun—and not Earth—stands at the center of the universe. Earth is just a planet, he said, whirling around the sun. But in the 1600s, most people still thought that this "revolutionary" idea was ridiculous.

This star map, made in 1660, shows some of the major star pictures, or constellations, seen in the Southern Hemisphere, including (bottom left) Leo, Cancer and Gemini.

that change the color, or mood, of the planets' influence. If the Sun is in the hot-tempered sign of Leo the Lion, its effect will be different than if it had wandered into the gloomy realm of Cancer the Crab. Since the planets are constantly zooming around—near and far, below and above—their rays reach us in gusts. As these cosmic winds bluster around us, we humans are blown to and fro. Is it any wonder that our journey through life is so unpredictable?

The job of an astrologer is to study these unruly energies by casting horoscopes. A horoscope is a diagram that shows the position of the star signs and planets as they appear from a particular place at a particular time. A horoscope of your birth, for example,

Old News

The idea that the stars and planets control our lives is extremely old. Magicians in ancient Babylonia (now Iraq) cast the first known horoscope in 410 B.C., almost 2500 years ago. The Babylonians also invented the twelve signs of the zodiac that William Lilly used and that are still found in the horoscope columns of our newspapers.

The Dark Art of Math

Astrologers were mathematicians as well as star-gazers. In casting horoscopes, they had to work out the angles between the planets and make other complicated calculations. Because math was used by magicians, many people worried that it might be one of the Dark Arts. Partly for that reason, math was not taught in schools or universities until the mid-1600s.

A midwife and two assistants help with the birth of a baby, sometime around 1550. In the background, a pair of astrologers are studying the position of the planets and stars and casting a horoscope for the newcomer.

would show all the heavenly forces that were beaming down on you when you took your first breath. If your parents had hired a wizard to cast such a chart, they could have requested a complete preview of your life. What would you do for a living? How many children would you have? The astrologer would have plotted planets, drawn lines, measured angles, worked out the math and then told your parents what to expect.

It took William Lilly eight solid weeks of study to master the art of casting horoscopes. By then, he was skilled enough to catch his teacher in an error. A woman had come to Evans with a question and, after drawing up her chart, he had assured her that everything would be fine. The woman paid him for this service and went merrily on her way. But Lilly could see at a glance that his master was wrong; the horoscope actually predicted nothing but trouble. Why had Evans mislead the woman, Lilly wanted to know. She wouldn't have paid him if he'd told her the truth, Evans snapped. Didn't Lilly know the first thing about practicing a magical craft?

But cheating was one of the tricks of the trade that Lilly preferred not to learn. So he canceled his classes with Evans and continued his studies alone. He perfected his skills as an astrologer by reading stacks of mysterious, tattered old books with titles like *Magia Naturalis* ("Natural Magic") and *Ars Notoria* ("Forbidden Arts"). The more he studied, the more dazzled Lilly became by the scope of his subject. The invisible beams from the heavens did far more than shape the ups and downs of our individual lives. They left their mark everywhere, on everything they touched. They were written in the lines on our forehead; they chose the position of our moles. They beamed their healing powers into herbs and precious stones. The whole magical universe was literally throbbing with heavenly influence. The truth really was out there, in the stars and planets.

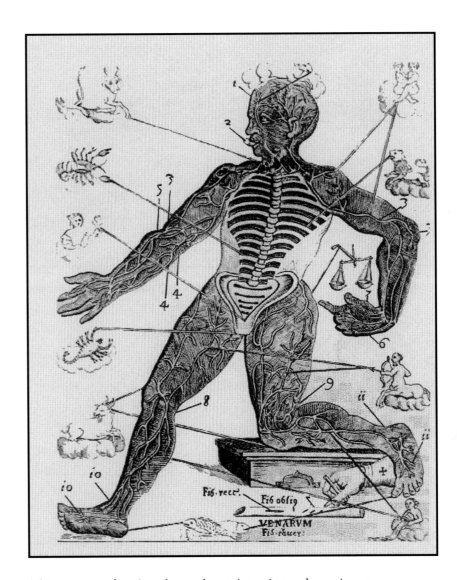

This cutaway drawing shows the major veins and arteries, as well as the star signs that are linked to various body parts. The influence of Sagittarius (the archer), for example, is felt by the thighs, while Libra (the scales) influences the hips. Astrologers—and even doctors—used charts like this to diagnose and treat illnesses.

THE PHILOSOPHER'S STONE

With many a sigh and many a groan,

They searched high and low for the magical stone.

For an aspiring wizard like Isaac Newton, astrology—wondrous though it was—was not the final frontier of magical knowledge. Beyond it, on the outer limits, lay the mysterious realm of the alchemists. Like astrologers, alchemists were wizards who used mathematics to study the magical forces in the natural world. But the alchemists were not content with just figuring out how Natural Magic worked. Instead, they wanted to gain control of the hidden powers that govern people's lives. A loving God could never have meant for people to suffer, the alchemists thought. If they could just fine-tune the magical system, they should be able to eliminate poverty and cure all sicknesses. They might even be able to defeat death.

The key to the alchemists' project was the philosopher's stone. This "stone" was usually described as a powder (sometimes yellow, but often red) that would cure all diseases and promote long life and health. And that was only the beginning of its astonishing powers.

Facing page: Alchemists were on the leading edge of wizardry. This illustration, from 1589, shows an alchemist brandishing a glass vessel and a banner of magical words, inside a frame of natural wonders.

Like astrologers, alchemists believed that rays from the stars and planets were important in their work. Here, an alchemist conducts experiments under the star sign of Aries the Ram. The apparatus at the left includes the alchemist's fireplace, or "cosmic furnace," and vessels and tubing made of glass.

Left: Two alchemists keep a close eye on the liquids and gases that are heating inside their elaborate glasswear.

The same miraculous substance could turn lead and other worthless metals into purest gold. Whoever knew the secret could simply, endlessly, make his own.

But there was one problem. The philosopher's stone was hidden somewhere in nature, and no one knew where to look. Some alchemists thought that it could be extracted from mixtures of minerals, such as sulfur and mercury. But others believed that it would be found inside some common object, something so ordinary that we would scarcely think it worth considering. It might be in egg shells, for example, or mint leaves or urine. So the alchemists set to work testing everything they could think of, each hoping to be the first to recover the priceless red dust.

An alchemist's laboratory was a phantasmagoria of strange sights and sounds. The heart of the operation was a large brick fireplace, or oven—the "cosmic furnace"—that provided heat for the experiments. In the red glow of the fire sat the alchemist or (if he could afford one) his assistant, sweating and squeezing away on a set of bellows. The puffing of the bellows kept the furnace supplied with air and helped to keep the fire at the right temperature. If it became too cool or flared too hot, the experiment was lost. On the hearth of the furnace stood a fantastically shaped vessel of pottery and blown glass, with a round body and

The Origins of Alchemy

Like astrology, alchemy is a very ancient art. Although nobody knows for sure who the first alchemists were, they were probably scholars and priests in ancient India and China. Over the centuries, alchemy was also practiced in Egypt (between about 300 B.C. and A.D. 600) and in Persia (from A.D. 600 to 1300). Alchemical knowledge came to Europe from Persia about eight hundred years ago (around A.D. 1200). At that time, a number of ancient alchemical texts were translated from Arabic into Latin, the language that was used by European scholars. As more Europeans learned about alchemy, the excitement grew. The search for the philosopher's stone was at its peak in the 1500s and 1600s.

The Motto of the Alchemists

Ora, Lege, Lege, Lege Relege, Labora, et Invenies. (Pray, read, read, read Reread, labor and succeed.)

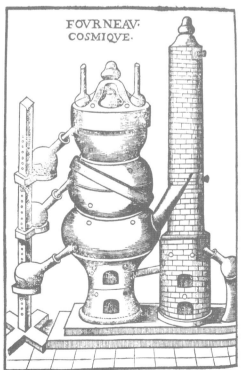

FOVRNEAV. COSMIQVE.

A boy watches in wonder as an alchemist tends one of his endless experiments. The alchemist is using bellows to puff air onto the fire in his furnace, trying to get the temperature just right. In the background, another experiment is already on the boil, while two assistants prepare ingredients for yet another trial. This view of an alchemist's laboratory was first published in 1650.

Left: "Fourneau cosmique" is French for "cosmic furnace."

a slender, tapering arm. This side tube (or tubes—there could be more than one) swelled out near its end to form a second round globe. The walls of the room were lined with other contorted shapes of glass, each one weirder than the last.

The alchemist used these wondrous vessels to search for the philosopher's stone through a process of heating and distillation. First, a sample of the material to be tested was mixed with other ingredients and placed in a sturdy bowl, or crucible. The mixture was then heated. If a high temperature was desired, the crucible was placed on the furnace. If a lower heat was preferred, it was put in a warm-water bath or wrapped in rotting horse manure. (The heat of decomposition kept the mixture warm.) Then, once the heating phase was completed, the distillation began. The baked-on material in the crucible was washed out with an acid and poured into a glass vessel. Then the vessel was sealed and put back on the fire. The temperature had to stay steady for a specified length of time, often for a "philosopher's month" of forty days. In due course, a fraction of the original mass would turn into a gas and rise up through the vessel and into the tubular arms. As the vapors began to cool, they would condense into droplets and collect at the ends of the tubes. This distillate could then be removed and dried into a powder. Had the philosopher's stone finally been discovered?

Sometimes the alchemist was guided in his experiments by his own experience, but often he followed instructions that he found in books. There were

Speaking in Riddles

Alchemists were a snooty lot, who thought that they were nobler and smarter than ordinary people. To make sure that the common folk couldn't understand their books, they described their experiments in riddles. Here, for example, is how a seventeenth-century alchemist named Basil Valentine described a method for purifying gold ("the King") by heating it with antimony sulfide ("the Wolf"). The goal was to produce pure gold ("Our Body") that could be used in future experiments: "Take a fierce grey Wolf. Cast to him the body of the King, and when he has devoured it, burn him entirely to ashes in a great fire. By this process the King will be liberated; and when it has been performed thrice the Lion has overcome the Wolf, who will find nothing more to devour in him. Thus Our Body has become rendered fit for the first stage of our work."

Above and right: Alchemists used all kinds of strange-looking glass vessels, including flasks known as the ostrich, the pelican and the bear.

shelves and shelves of alchemical texts (some more than a thousand years old), and no two of them recommended exactly the same procedure. Yet each author insisted that, if you followed his instructions precisely, you were guaranteed to succeed. Combine this and that, stir and heat, distill, extract, take a pinch of the resulting powder, throw it into a pot full of lead and—presto-chango—you would have untold riches.

Yet time after time, the powder didn't work, and time after time, there was some excuse. The assistant had let the fire go out before the forty days were up or a glass vessel had shattered part way through the distillation. And even if the alchemist did manage to complete every step, he still might fail because of his own spiritual weakness. At the same time as he was purifying liquids in his laboratory, he was expected to be purifying his soul with prayer and fasting. After all, God wouldn't reveal his deepest truths to a common sinner!

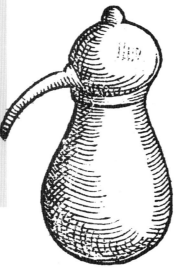

For one reason and another, the philosopher's stone had always stayed out of reach. Yet the alchemists remained confident that they would succeed. Their hopes were kept alive by stories of people (usually in some far-distant time or place) who had accomplished the ultimate magic. There was Nicholas Flamel, for example, a clerk who had lived in Paris around 1400. Apparently, he had learned the secret of the philosopher's stone from a mysterious old book and, with his

Their clothes in tatters and their faces strained, an alchemist and his assistant pursue their research amid a clutter of broken flasks and discarded tools.

wife Perrenelle, had literally made a fortune in pure gold. They had used their sudden wealth to build three churches and fourteen hospitals in various parts of France. Yet, remarkably, their achievement had gone unnoticed for two hundred years, and their alchemical knowledge appeared to have died with them. We might never have known about them if it hadn't been for a pamphlet that appeared out of the blue in the early 1600s. This booklet was presented as the autobiography of Nicholas Flamel, and who could doubt a story that came from the man himself?

There were many other eyewitness accounts. Dr. Arthur Dee, who lived from 1579 to 1651, was a respected physician who served both the czar of Russia and the king of England. An alchemist—and the son of the wizard John Dee—he swore on oath

How did he do that? The man on the right is so astonished by the magician's sleight of hand that he does not notice the boy (the magician's son?) who is picking his pocket. This painting, which is probably by the great Dutch artist Hieronymus Bosch, dates from around 1500.

that he had seen the philosopher's stone with his own eyes, "ocularly, undeceivably, and frequently," when he was a boy. In fact, he remembered playing darts with a piece of gold that had been drawn from the alchemical furnace.

One of Arthur Dee's contemporaries, Jean Baptiste van Helmont, was a careful observer of nature and the person who invented the concept of a gas. He was also an alchemist. In his autobiography, which was published in 1662, he wrote about an Irishman named Butler who had "a certain little stone" that could be used to treat illnesses. "I saw a poor old woman, a laundress, who from 16 years or thereabouts laboured with an intolerable migraine, presently cured in my presence," van Helmont said. To accomplish this small miracle, Butler had first dipped his stone in a spoonful of oil and then had poured the "treated" oil into a small bottle of regular olive oil. He had taken one drop of this diluted mixture and placed it on the woman's forehead. She was "straightway cured and remained whole for some years," van Helmont marveled, "the which I attest."

In another time and another place, the philosopher's stone would be written off as a wonderful fantasy. But, in the 1600s, it was on the cutting edge of wizardry.

Tricky Business

Alchemy lent itself to trickery. A fake alchemist set himself up to look as much as possible like the real thing. But he also had a secret piece of equipment—a lump of charcoal or a stirring stick with a hollow center. This hollow could be filled with gold and sealed with black wax. In the heat of the furnace, the wax would melt and the gold spill out. It was magic, without a doubt!

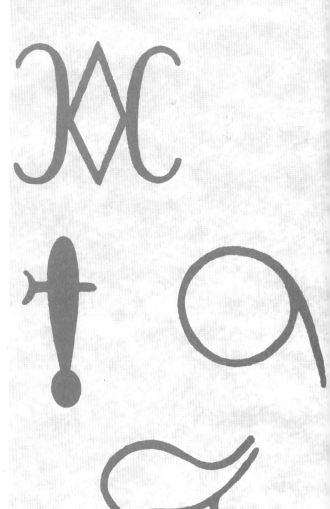

THE MAKING OF A MAGUS

One wave of history's magic wand—

Tomorrow's here and the past is gone.

I n a universe that was pulsing with mysteries, one thing had become perfectly clear. Nothing and no one could ever turn Isaac Newton into a farmer. He'd been hopeless at sixteen, when he'd left school and, even with time and experience, his farm work had never improved. Eventually, his family gave up in despair and sent him to college.

By 1669, the one-time boy wizard had grown to be a young man of twenty-seven. An accomplished mathematician, he had recently won himself a place at Cambridge University as a "fellow," or research scholar. This position entitled him to a room in a vine-covered residence, meals at the "high table" in the faculty dining room, an annual allowance for academic gowns and a comfortable wage. In return, his only duties were to study, to think, to dream—to follow his curiosity wherever it might lead. Even his mean-spirited relatives were finally forced to admit that Isaac the Failed Farmer had made something of himself.

This painting from a storybook published in 1911 shows an alchemist in his moment of wonderment and success. He has made gold!

Facing page: Surrounded by glittering flasks, this storybook wizard, from 1912, fixes his strange, glassy stare on the mysteries in his crystal ball.

An alchemist's flasks glow with his latest discovery. Although he may not have found the philosopher's stone, he may quite possibly have made a useful contribution to chemical knowledge.

Isaac's first response to his good fortune was to brighten up his room with a splash of crimson red: new cushions, chairs, curtains and bedspreads. His second move was to set himself up as an alchemist. Soon, his freshly redecorated quarters were crammed with beakers, flasks, crucibles, tubes, stocks of chemicals—mercury, silver and lead—and a chaos of books and papers. Somehow, he also managed to wedge in two alchemical furnaces. Like the boy who had once crouched behind the counter in Mr. Clark's shop to watch hidden powers at work, he now bent over his alchemical experiments to see what secrets he could uncover.

His alchemy quickly became a total obsession. When his experiments were running, he forgot to take his meals and scarcely bothered to sleep. His whole attention was focused on keeping the fires burning and observing what was happening inside his flasks. Wizard that he was, he spoke about the chemicals in his vessels almost as if they were alive. If two substances, like oil and water, refused to mix together, it was because they suffered from a "secret principle of unsociableness." (They didn't like each other.) If they reacted with each other, like the metals lead and antimony, it was because one of them was a "magnet" that attracted the other to it. (They were good friends.) From the beginning, Isaac had believed that invisible forces were at work in the natural world. When his flasks began to fizz or steam or glow, he could see those magical powers at work.

A hush fell over Isaac as he considered the mysteries that he held in his hands. This was profound research and deserved to be kept secret. So, although he made careful notes about his experiments—some 7000 pages in all—he didn't discuss his alchemy with anyone except his closest friends. And yet he labored on. Finally, in 1693, after twenty-four years of effort, he noted in his private papers that he had found the philosopher's stone and succeeded in making gold.

An (Al)chemical Reaction

Alchemy was the ancestor of chemistry. As scientists, the chemists threw out all the magical talk about "attractions" and "unsociability." They looked at atoms and molecules as simple building blocks. In time, they discovered that atoms themselves are made up of smaller particles—protons, neutrons and electrons. By tinkering with these sub-atomic particles, chemists now have the ability to achieve the alchemists' cherished goal. Although it would be costly, they could turn lead into pure gold.

Making a Mint

In the late 1600s when he was middle aged, Isaac Newton abandoned all his magical and scientific studies and took a job running the Royal Mint. Here he was able to apply the knowledge of metals and metallurgy that he had acquired through his studies of alchemy. Although he never succeeded in making alchemical gold (except perhaps in his dreams), he did literally make bags and bags of money!

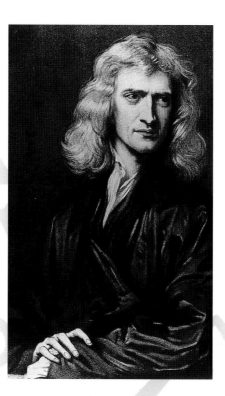

Left: This portrait of Isaac Newton, at age forty-six, shows him looking gaunt and baggy-eyed from lack of food and rest—the very picture of an alchemist.

Magic and Science

Many people think of magic and science as opposites, like right and wrong. As these people tell the story, humanity sat under a cloud of error for thousands of years, until science finally came along and showed us how the world worked. They think of science as the enemy of magic. But, in fact, science and magic are more like members of a family. They do not always agree with each other, but they share the same ancestry. Most of the people who contributed to the Scientific Revolution were wizards as well as scientists. In addition to Isaac Newton, the list includes the astronomers Nicolas Copernicus and Johannes Kepler and the chemist Robert Boyle. Magic introduced them to the study of mathematics and the search for hidden truths. In a sense, the rise of science was the surprising last chapter in the wizards' quest for understanding.

He then immediately suffered a nervous breakdown. When he recovered, he packed up all his equipment, put his papers in boxes and trunks, and abandoned his research. No one breathed a word about his alchemical work during the rest of his long life. (He died at the age of eighty-four in 1727.) In fact, his secrets remained safe until 1936, when a chest full of his private writings turned up for sale at an auction and were finally made available to the public.

When news got round that the great Sir Isaac Newton had been an alchemist, many people were deeply shocked. By this time, he had gone down in history as a brilliant physicist and one of the leading figures in the Scientific Revolution. Not only had he invented a powerful new kind of mathematics known as calculus, he had also revolutionized the science of optics (the study of light and lenses). As if that weren't enough, he had developed the first mathematical formulas for calculating the energy of objects in motion. To Newton the magician, the world had been buzzing with vitality. To Newton the scientist, it looked more like a machine. His formulas described a simple, mechanical universe in which lifeless objects exchanged physical energy. Welcome to the world of modern physics.

For Isaac Newton, there was no contradiction between magic and science. He believed that the two ways of understanding the world complemented each other. (If he had summarized his thoughts in a formula, it might have read: Magic + science = truth.) But many people around him were awe-struck by

In the new age of science, people who believed in magic were thought to be fools. This illustration, which dates from the 1700s, shows the devil (right) slipping a dunce cap onto a man who has consulted a sorceress.

his scientific achievements. They thought he had learned to read God's thoughts. To these people, his work marked the triumph of science and the death of magic. Wizards had made a lot of fabulous claims, but what had they ever done? Had they captured a unicorn? Had they found the philosopher's stone? Suddenly, the whole, proud magical tradition began to look like two thousand years of foolish errors. The wizards' ideas may have been amusing or even inspiring, but what good was that? The most important thing, the skeptics said, was to be correct.

Isaac Newton's science had one great strength. It worked. Soon, his physics had opened the door on a new age of wonders. The steam engine, the locomotive, the internal combustion engine, the jet plane, the rocket ship—all these miracles of technology would eventually become possible by using Newton's mathematics. Magicians had dreamed of flying, but for them it was only a dream. In the new world of science, dreams became reality.

The Scientific Revolution of the 1500s and 1600s marked a dramatic change in the way that people understood the world. After that, science moved into the lead, and wizardry was no longer taken seriously. Yet, even today, magical ideas are all around us, in stories, in music, in art—in our sense that the

Left: A group of children taunt and jeer at an old man whom they suspect of being a wizard.

Right: The world of wizards and wizardry lives on in storybooks. This recent image of a sorcerer was painted by Robin Muller for his book *The Sorcerer's Apprentice.* Though delightfully fresh and original, it borrows freely from old drawings of apothecaries, astrologers and especially alchemists.

Below: The wonderful Wizard of Oz was conjured up by the writer L. Frank Baum in 1900. This portrait, based on "the Wizard's latest photographs taken by the Royal Photographer of Oz" (or so we're told), was drawn by John R. Neill.

natural world is brimming with secrets. Surprising as it may seem, there is even a hint of magic in science.

Isaac Newton's scientific masterpiece was a book called *The Mathematical Principles of Natural History*, which he published in 1687. In it, he extends the laws of physics out into the universe, to describe the movement of the stars and planets. At the center of his theory lies the concept of gravity. This force is important to us because it holds us on Earth and helps to keep all the planets in their orbits around the sun. Newton used mathematics to show how gravity operated, but he wasn't sure what it was. Could it be, the old wizard wondered, that it was an occult, or hidden, force—an unexplained attraction between the planets? If he had not been trained in magic, he would probably never have thought of anything as strange as a gravitational force.

To this day, scientists cannot say exactly how gravity works. Is there still a touch of magic at the heart of our universe?

"The Great Ocean of Truth"

Isaac Newton was modest about his accomplishments. "I know not what I appear to the world," he once wrote, "but to myself I seem to have been only like a boy playing on the sea-shore, and diverting myself in now and then finding a smoother pebble or a prettier shell, whilst the great ocean of truth lay all undiscovered before me."

Glossary

Alchemist: a person who practices alchemy

Alchemy: a mystical, magical art that involved experimenting with chemical reactions in the hope of discovering the philosopher's stone

Amulet: a magical charm that is worn as a necklace or bracelet

Antipathies: dislikes, repulsions

Apothecary: a person who sells potions and charms, as well as ingredients for making them

Astrologer: a person who practices astrology

Astrology: the magical art of calculating the influence of the planets and stars on people's lives. Astrology is based on the idea that radiation from the heavens affects what happens on Earth.

Black Magic: evil magic. *See also* Dark Arts

Calculus: a mathematical method for studying graphs or objects that follow a curved path

Charm: a magical phrase or verse

Charmer: a village healer

Chemistry: the science that studies what substances are made of and how they interact with each other

Conjure: cause to appear

Constellation: a group of stars that can be linked into a join-the-dots picture. *See also* Star sign

Cosmic furnace: a kind of fireplace, or stove, that was used by alchemists in their experiments

Dark Arts: evil magic, practiced with the assistance of the devil

Demon: evil spirit

Distillation: the process of purifying substances through evaporation and condensation

Distillate: a substance that is left after distillation

Divination: the magical art of seeing into the past and the future

Diviner: a person who practices divination

Doctrine of signatures: the idea that the appearance of a plant provided a clue to how the plant was meant to be used

Familiar spirit: a demon in the shape of a pet animal

Fixed stars: stars. *See also* Wandering stars

Herb: a plant, especially one that is used in medicine or in cooking

Horoscope: a chart drawn up by an astrologer to calculate the influence of the stars and planets on a particular person at a particular time and place

Magic: a way of understanding the world based on the idea that the natural world is alive with invisible forces. The practice of magic is the art of controlling these forces. *See also* Science

Magus: a great wizard who has a deep understanding of hidden realities. The plural of "magus" is "magi."

Matter: anything that takes up space (a solid, liquid or gas)

Natural Magic: the art of working with invisible powers that are hidden in the natural world

Occult: hidden; in a general sense, occult means anything mysterious or magical

Oracle: something or someone that speaks about the hidden world, especially the future

Pact: a deal or contract

Philosopher: a person who thinks deeply about the meaning of life

Philosopher's stone: a magical substance that was supposed to cure all diseases and turn worthless metals into gold. Finding the philosopher's stone was the goal of alchemy.

Physics: the science that deals with energy and matter and how they interact with each other

Plague: a terrible epidemic disease that killed thousands of people in Europe in the 1600s. It is also called bubonic plague and the Black Death.

Possessed: invaded by demons. People used to think that demons were the cause of mental illness.

Potion: a mixture of herbs and other ingredients believed to have magical powers

Radiation: pulses or beams of energy that travel through space

Science: a way of understanding the world based on the assumption that the physical world is governed by physical forces. *See also* Magic

Scientific Revolution: a dramatic change in the way people understood the world, which took place in the 1500s and 1600s. During the Scientific Revolution, magic was discredited and modern science began to advance. The leading figures in this movement included Nicolas Copernicus, Galileo Galilei, Francis Bacon, Rene Descartes and Isaac Newton.

Scryer: a person who sees the future in a crystal ball or some other reflective surface. The art of the scryer is called scrying.

Sorcerer: an evil magician, a practitioner of the Dark Arts

Spirit: a living energy

Star sign: one of twelve constellations (pictures found in the stars) that are used by astrologers

Sympathies: friendships, attractions

Virtue: strength

Wandering stars: planets

Witch: a person, usually a woman, who has made a deal with the devil and gained the power to perform evil magic

Witch bottle: a pottery bottle that was buried under a door step or wall of a house to protect the residents from witches. Witch bottles were also used to break evil spells.

Wizard: a skilled magician

Zodiac: a circular diagram representing the heavens that features the twelve star signs used by astrologers

FOR MORE INFORMATION

THE MAGICAL TRADITION

Websites

- The Alchemy Website and Virtual Library (www.levity.com/ alchemy/home.html) provides a complete on-line guide to alchemical books, symbols, quotations and discussion groups. You will even find self-study courses on the practice of alchemy.

- *Natural Magick* by John Baptist Porta was first published in Latin in 1558 and translated into English in 1658. If you want to find out more about what wizards really thought and did, you can read this book on the Web. Go to www.members.tscnet.com/pages/ omard1/jportat5.html or search for the phrase "natural magick."

- The John Dee Society (www.johndee.org) focuses on the life of a great English scholar and wizard. The John Dee Publication Project (www.dnai.com/cholden/) provides the complete texts of diaries John Dee kept about his attempts to communicate with angels and to learn their language.

- The Twilit Grotto Esoteric Archives (www.esotericarchives.com/ esoteric.htm) is a huge, on-line library of magical texts, most of which were first published in the 1500s and 1600s. Among many others, it includes a work in four volumes called *On Occult Philosophy* by Henry Cornelius Agrippa. This is one of the standard books on Natural Magic. The archives also includes a selection of "grimoires," or spell books.

Novels

There are hundreds, perhaps even thousands, of novels that explore the magical tradition in one way and another. Here are a handful of recommended titles:

- *The Boggart* by Susan Cooper (Macmillan McElderry, 1993) is a rollicking tale about the misadventures of a mythical creature from the Highlands of Scotland who is forced to cope in the modern technological world. Susan Cooper is also the author of the much-loved "Dark Is Rising Series," which includes five books: *Over Sea, Over Stone*; *The Dark Is Rising*; *Greenwitch*; *The Grey Tree* and *Silver on the Tree*.

- *Harry Potter and the Philosopher's Stone* is the first in a wonderful series of novels by J. K. Rowling. (It was published in the United States as *Harry Potter and the Sorcerer's Stone*.) Apart from the fun and excitement of the stories, it is fascinating to see how the author weaves elements from the magical tradition into her fiction.

- *A Break With Charity: A Story About the Salem Witch Trials* by Ann Rinaldi (Harcourt Brace, Jovanovich, 1992) examines events in Salem, Massachusetts, in 1692, where a group of young girls find themselves at the center of a vicious controversy about witchcraft.

- *The Magician's Apprentice* by Tom McGowen (E. P. Dutton, 1987) follows Tigg and his magician friend Armindor as they attempt to recover the lost wisdom from the Age of Magic. Who is trying to frustrate their search?

- *Redwork* by Michael Bedard (Lester, 1990) is an engrossing novel that focuses on thirteen-year-old Cass and his mysterious neighbor Mr. Magnus. Could he have some distant connection to Albertus Magnus, the medieval alchemist?

- *The Wonderful Wizard of Oz* by L. Frank Baum was first published in 1900 and has been in print ever since. The title character is a magician who is only able to work wonders because people believe in him. If you like the book, you may also enjoy some of its sequels: there are fourteen in all. And, of course, there's also the classic 1939 movie version, starring Judy Garland.

Reference Books

- *The Good Spell Book: Love Charms, Magical Cures and Other Practical Sorcery* by Gillian Kemp (Little, Brown, 2000) provides instructions for magically curing headaches, finding lost pets, easing cramps and solving any number of other everyday problems. Does her magic work? See for yourself.

- *Witches and Magic-Makers* by Douglas Hill (Dorling Kindersley, 1997) is a lively, pictorial book about the practice of magic around the world. Subjects range from "Famous witches and wizards" to "African sorcery" and "Southeast Asian magic."

ISAAC NEWTON AND THE SCIENTIFIC REVOLUTION

Websites

- Newton.org.uk (www.newton.org.uk) offers a virtual museum about the life and work of Sir Isaac Newton, including biographical notes, maps, portraits and links to other related sites. This site provides reliable information about Newton's contribution to science, but it neglects his interest in magic.

- The Newton Institute at Cambridge University (www.newton.cam.ac.uk/newton.html) provides links to a variety of high-quality sites about Sir Isaac Newton's life and his contributions to science. Look for the headings "Isaac Newton Resources" and "Isaac Newton on the Web."

- The Modern History Sourcebook (www.fordham.edu/halsall/mod/SCIREV.html.) offers a brief summary in note form of the main events in the Scientific Revolution. For a more detailed and advanced account, check out a site entitled "Scientific Revolution" written by Professor Gerhard Rempel of Western New England College.

Reference Books

- *Isaac Newton and the Scientific Revolution* by Gale E. Christianson (Oxford University Press, 1998) is a thoughtful account of Isaac Newton's life and work, written at a young-adult level.

- *Isaac Newton: Discovering the Laws that Govern the Universe* by Michael White (Blackbird Press, 1999) is a brief, illustrated account of Isaac Newton's scientific work, especially for young readers. Sadly, the author does not mention Newton's interest in magic.

- *Isaac Newton and Gravity* by Steve Parker (Chelsea House, 1995) is another book that covers much the same ground.

A Note on Sources

Picture Credits

The facts of Isaac Newton's life that are presented in this book are drawn from Richard Westfall's *Never at Rest: A Biography of Isaac Newton* (1980). In its 908 pages, this book covers every aspect of Newton's personal and intellectual career. Michael White's *Isaac Newton: The Last Sorcerer* (1997) was also useful, particularly for its explanations of Newton's scientific, magical and theological ideas. The basic source on Newton's practice of alchemy is *The Janus Face of Genius: The Role of Alchemy in Newton's Thought* by Betty Jo Teeter Dobbs (1991).

All the incidents in Newton's life that are described in these pages—his miserable home life, friendship with Mr. Clark, early interest in the apothecary's art, introduction to astrology and devotion to alchemy—are historically accurate. The suggestion that the young Newton wanted to be a wizard is speculation. That he eventually became one is a well-established fact.

There is a huge amount of scholarly literature on the practice of magic in early modern Europe. Frances Yates's study *The Occult Philosophy in the Elizabethan Age* (1979) offers an overview of the position of magic in Renaissance thought. Other valuable sources, which were used in the preparation of this book, include *John Dee: The World of an Elizabethan Magus* by Peter J. French (1972); *John Dee's Natural Philosophy: Between Science and Religion* by Nicholas H. Clulee (1988); and *Occult and Scientific Mentalities in the Renaissance,* edited by Brian Vickers (1984). Lynn Thorndike's *A History of*

Magic and Experimental Science (1941) surveys the subject in eight, detailed volumes. The place of magic in everyday life is covered in Keith Thomas's thorough and captivating *Religion and the Decline of Magic* (1972). Witchcraft and the Renaissance witch craze are discussed in *Witch: The Wild Ride from Wicked to Wicca* (2000) by Candace Savage.

The Dark Arts are the subject of Richard Kieckhefer's highly recommended book *Forbidden Rites: A Necromancer's Manual of the Fifteenth Century* (1997). Despite its age, C. J. S. Thompson's *The Mystery and Art of the Apothecary* (1929) remains a first-rate source of information on healing magic. The history of alchemy is recounted in *The Alchemists: Founders of Modern Chemistry* by F. Sherwood Taylor (1952) and *Through Alchemy to Chemistry* by John Read (1957). Seventeenth-century astrology is covered in *The Last of the Astrologers* by William Lilly, edited by Katharine M. Briggs (1974) and *Familiar to All: William Lilly and Astrology in the Seventeenth Century* by Derek Parker (1975). All of the magical arts are surveyed in Kurt Seligman's *The History of Magic: A Catalogue of Sorcery, Witchcraft and the Occult* (1949, 1997).

INDEX